D1758009

DISCARDED

014173803 8

SUPER FOOD

AVOCADO

BLOOMSBURY
LONDON · OXFORD · NEW YORK · NEW DELHI · SYDNEY

CONTENTS

INTRODUCTION

'In the centre of the fruit
is a seed like a peeled chestnut.
And between this and the rind
is the part which is eaten,
which is abundant, and
is a paste similar to butter
and of very good taste.'

Gonzalo Fernandez de Oviedo
*Sumario de la Natural Historia
de las Indias*, 1526

HISTORY

Avocados originated in Mexico, where archaeological evidence shows them being gathered and eaten around 10,000 years ago. The tribes of Mesoamerica began to cultivate them from around 7,000 years ago.

The Aztec name for the avocado was 'ahuacatl', meaning testicle, a reference to the shape of the fruit and also to its reputed aphrodisiac qualities.

At the start of the 16th century the first Europeans arrived in the Americas and discovered a host of exotic new fruits. The first written mention of the avocado comes from explorer Martín Fernández de Enciso who, in his book *Summa de Geografía* (1519), described a fruit he had seen in Colombia: '... here are groves of many different sorts of edible fruits, among others is one which looks like an orange, and when it is ready for eating it turns yellowish; that which it contains is like butter and is of marvellous flavour, so good and pleasing to the palate that it is a marvellous thing.' That same year the historian Gonzalo Fernandez de Oviedo travelled with the famous explorer Cortez, and wrote about avocados in his *Natural History of the Indies*, published in 1526, noting that they were 'excellent when eaten with cheese'. The Spanish translated 'ahuacatl' as 'aguacate', and bought this new fruit back to the Old World with them.

As the explorers pushed inland the avocado began to spread to other parts of the Americas, and eventually it arrived on the island of Jamaica. When the British took back control of Jamaica from the Spanish the avocado came to their attention.

In 1657 a London publication describing Jamaica mentions 'Avocatas, a wholesome, pleasant fruit; in season in August, and sold for eight pence per piece.' This was expensive – avocados were obviously a novelty food. The next reference in English came in a 1672 work by William Hughes entitled *The American Physician: Or a treatise of the Roots, Plants, Trees, Shrubs, Fruit, Herbs & growing in the English Plantations in America*, where he gives a fuller description of what he called 'the Spanish Pear ... or the Shell-Pear'. He speculates that the names given to the fruit are due to it being planted by Spaniards, or a reference to the shell-like or 'crusty' peel.

When Sir Hans Sloane, the renowned physician and collector, catalogued Jamaican plants in 1696, he referred to the fruit as an 'avocado' for the first time. (He also called it the 'alligator pear-tree' in reference to the rough scaly skin of the fruit.)

The avocado was by now widespread throughout the Americas. George Washington visited Barbados in 1751 and noted the popularity of 'agovago pears'. During the 19th century avocado trees began to be planted in California, primarily by collectors of rare plants. An early assessment of the viability of commercial crops concluded that there was no prospect of them succeeding due

IN 1657 A LONDON PUBLICATION DESCRIBING JAMAICA MENTIONS 'AVOCATAS, A WHOLESOME, PLEASANT FRUIT: IN SEASON IN AUGUST, AND SOLD FOR EIGHT PENCE PER PIECE'.

to their lack of sweetness. However crops and varieties of avocado continued to be experimented with, and the first meeting of the Californian

> *George Washington visited Barbados in 1751 and noted the popularity of 'agovago pears'.*

avocado growers took place in 1915 with a stern admonition not to use the term 'alligator pear' again – the 'avocado' had arrived! Crops were also grown in Florida and Hawaii, although initially interest was localised.

During the 1950s the popularity of the avocado really took off, when it began to be included in salads. In the 1960s and 1970s the avocado featured in sophisticated British cuisine as 'an unusual ingredient for hors d'oevres' (*Mrs Beeton's Cookery and Household Management*, 1966), commonly paired with prawns and salad dressing. Not to mention being a colour inspiration for a generation of bathroom suites ...

Today, the avocado has been rediscovered and reinvented by a generation of well-informed and inspired foodies. Mexico, the spiritual home of the avocado, remains the biggest producer, however avocados are grown and enjoyed all over the world from California to New Zealand.

Avocados are now an indispensable component of modern cooking. The versatility of this amazing fruit means it can be used in a wide range of recipes including dips and salads, drinks, main courses and puddings. Recognised for their nutritional and health benefits, avocados are also utilised in beauty products and treatments as they contain skin-boosting vitamins and oils.

HEALTH BENEFITS

Avocados contain a highly beneficial range of around 20 minerals and vitamins which are essential to good health. Although they have a high fat content (a medium avocado contains significantly more calories than a Mars bar), this fat is the right kind of fat – mono-saturated fat – which helps reduce high cholesterol levels and thus lower the risk of heart disease and stroke.

Avocados are a good source of dietary fibre, soluble and insoluble, essential to effective digestion and to maintaining bowel health. Soluble fibre slows down the breakdown of carbohydrates so that your body feels fuller for longer, aiding weight loss by suppressing the urge to eat too often.

Avocados contain good quantities of folic acid which has been shown to decrease the risk of heart disease and stroke. It is also beneficial to pregnant women as it cuts the risk of neural birth defects in the foetus.

Folic acid also helps combat depression and facilitates good sleep and appetite. In addition, avocados contain potassium which also fights depression and fatigue, as well as regulating heart rate and blood pressure and aiding digestion. One avocado contains more potassium than a banana.

Avocados contain several important vitamins including Vitamins C, E, K, B5 and B6. Vitamin K supports good bone health and helps your blood to clot properly, while Vitamin E boosts the immune system and is essential

for good skin health. Avocados also contain traces of the minerals iron, copper, magnesium and manganese, which your body uses to strengthen bones, keep the heart healthy and produce red blood cells.

Avocados are known to be a nutrient booster, which means they help your body better absorb nutrients, such as carotenoids, in other vegetables.

Your skin is also protected by the antioxidants contained in avocados including beta-carotene, Vitamin C and Vitamin E, which protect against sun exposure and environmental damage, thus preventing wrinkles and slowing down signs of ageing. The oleic acid contained in avocados is also excellent for skin regeneration.

Avocados are great for your eyes as well, due to the antioxidants lutein and zeaxanthin, which protect against macular degeneration and cataracts.

With all these amazing benefits, we should be including avocados in our diet every day. Luckily they also taste great so this is not difficult to achieve. Try out some of the recipes in this book and enjoy this super food!

RECIPES

*'I think it to be one of the most rare
and most pleasant Fruits in that Island:
it nourisheth and strengtheneth the
body, corroborating the vital spirits,
and procuring lust exceedingly: the Pulp
being taken out and macerated in some
convenient thing, and eaten with a little
Vinegar and Pepper, or several other
ways, is very delicious meat.'*

William Hughes
*The American Physician: Or a treatise
of the Roots, Plants, Trees, Shrubs,
Fruit, Herbs & growing in the English
Plantations in America,* 1672

SERVES: 2
PREPARATION: 5 MINUTES

BREAKFAST SMOOTHIES

You can blend pretty much anything you like with an avocado to make a delicious smoothie as its creamy taste provides a great base ingredient.

INGREDIENTS

- ½ ripe avocado
- 100ml mango chunks
- a handful of spinach leaves
- 200ml apple juice
- 1 tsp chia seeds

MANGO & SPINACH

This super-healthy smoothie combines avocado and mango with raw spinach and nutritious chia seeds for a refreshing start to the day.

Just place all the ingredients in a blender and whizz until fully combined.

Pour into a glass and enjoy!

INGREDIENTS

- ½ ripe avocado
- 1 pear
- 1 banana
- a small handful of blueberries
- a thumb-sized piece of ginger
- 250ml almond milk

BLUEBERRY, GINGER & PEAR

Blueberries are packed with antioxidants, while fresh ginger root aids digestion. Blend them with avocado, pear and banana for a deliciously creamy smoothie.

SERVES: 2
PREPARATION: **5 MINUTES**
COOKS IN: **12 MINUTES**

INGREDIENTS

- 1 ripe avocado
- 2 eggs
- 2 rashers of cooked smoked bacon, cut into small pieces
- salt and freshly ground black pepper
- a handful of chopped chives

 TOP TIP

Use good quality free-range eggs for maximum protein, omega 3 oils and vitamins.

BACON & EGG BAKED AVOCADO

The classic combination of egg and crispy bacon served inside an avocado provides a quick and easy meal.

METHOD

Preheat oven to 220ºC/425ºF/gas 7.

Cut the avocado in half and carefully remove the stone. You don't need to peel it. Scoop out a bit more flesh to create holes big enough for the eggs.

Place the avocado halves in a dish which will hold them securely so the egg doesn't spill while cooking.

Crack one of the eggs and carefully fill the hole in one of the avocado halves, then repeat with the other egg. Scatter the bacon pieces on top, and season with salt and freshly ground black pepper.

Bake for 12 minutes depending on how you like your eggs.

Sprinkle with the chives and serve.

MAKES: 12 BROWNIES
PREPARATION: 5 MINUTES
COOKS IN: 30 MINUTES

CHOCOLATE
BROWNIES

These brownies use the naturally healthy fat of avocados as a replacement for butter, and make a great mid-morning snack.

INGREDIENTS

- 200g plain flour
- 1 tsp baking powder
- 100g light brown sugar
- 50g cocoa powder
- 1 large ripe avocado, mashed well
- 2 eggs
- 100g dark chocolate, smashed into pieces (or you could use prepared chunks)

METHOD

Preheat oven to 180°C/350°F/gas 4.

Combine the dry ingredients in a bowl.
In a separate bowl beat the egg and avocado together thoroughly before pouring into the dry mix. Blend well and finally add the chunks of chocolate.

Spread out on a greased baking tray to a depth of 2cm.

Bake for 30 minutes until the tops are crispy and the insides ooze with melted chocolate.

AVOCADOS CONTAIN POTASSIUM WHICH FIGHTS DEPRESSION AND FATIGUE, AS WELL AS REGULATING HEART RATE AND BLOOD PRESSURE AND AIDING DIGESTION.

SOUP

SERVES: 2
PREPARATION: 10 MINUTES
COOKS IN: 10 MINUTES

Although you can cook avocados, they are best eaten raw in order to protect their nutritional benefits which can be damaged by heat. In traditional Mexican cuisine uncooked avocado is often added to a cooked dish, and this is the approach taken in this simple flavoursome soup.

INGREDIENTS

- 1 tbsp olive oil
- 1 onion, chopped
- 2 cloves garlic, finely chopped
- 400g tin chopped tomatoes
- 300ml chicken stock
- 1 tbsp tomato purée
- 2 tsp sugar
- ½ tbsp chilli powder
- salt and freshly ground black pepper
- 2 ripe avocados, peeled
- 100g cooked chicken breast, shredded
- crème fraiche and croutons, to serve

METHOD

Sauté the onion gently in the olive oil until translucent, stirring frequently. Add the garlic and cook for a further minute.

Pour in the tomatoes with the stock, tomato purée, sugar and chilli powder and bring to the boil. Simmer for five to ten minutes. Add salt and freshly ground black pepper to taste.

Remove the pan from the heat and leave to cool. Chop 1½ of the avocados into chunks, add to the pan and blend until smooth. Stir in the shredded chicken breast and gently reheat the soup.

To serve, finely slice the remaining half of the avocado. Place the soup in bowls and arrange the slices on top, with a swirl of crème fraiche and some croutons scattered over it.

WHY ISN'T THE AVOCADO EXTINCT?

The avocado tree grows its fruit to attract giant megafauna that died out thousands of years ago ...

Plants survive by spreading their seeds in a variety of ways including a method of dispersal called *endozoochory*, where animals eat the seeds and carry them until they are excreted undamaged far from the original plant. In this way the new seedlings aren't competing with the parent plant for light and nutrients. In order to tempt animals to eat them, botanic fruits have developed a nutritious flesh around their seeds, so the system is mutually beneficial to animal and plant. The animal gets a good meal; the plant propagates.

> *The avocado's huge stone is significantly larger than that of most fruits... So what animal could eat and disperse the seed of an avocado?*

In order to aid digestion, the avocado stone is slippery for ease of swallowing, but also mildly toxic and bitter-tasting to deter animals from chewing it. Its huge size would present a choking hazard to most animals alive today. So what animal could eat and disperse the seed of an avocado? The evolutionary biologists Daniel Janzen and Paul Martin studied the forests of Central America in the 1980s and found around 40 examples of plants which have puzzling seed dispersal traits that suggest their dependence on animals now long disappeared. They coined the term 'evolutionary anachronism' to describe species including the avocado which have co-evolved to be eaten by animals that have been extinct for thousands of years.

The avocado had evolved a reproductive method aimed at enormous herbivores roaming the planet millions of years ago. The fruit only ripens after it has fallen from the tree, a tactic developed to attract the animals grazing nearby. The megafauna of the Cenozoic era, such as the giant ground sloth, mammoths, and the oddly-named gomphotheres, would have had no problem swallowing the massive avocado stone as they ate the fruit. By relying on this megafaunal dispersal syndrome the avocado flourished, as Connie Barlow states in her article *Haunting the Wild Avocado*, 'Wave upon wave of Cenozoic megafauna faithfully harvested avocado fruits, season upon season, for tens of millions of years'.

13,000 years ago huge climactic changes marked the end of the Pleistocene epoch and there was a mass extinction of species from the face of the planet. The giant ground sloth and the gomphotheres were among the many huge and strange creatures lost forever.

'Wave upon wave of Cenozoic megafauna faithfully harvested avocado fruits, season upon season, for tens of millions of years.'

Without the large mammals to ingest and spread its seed, the avocado should have followed them into extinction. However the avocado did survive, and Connie Barlow says that '... the avocado is clueless that the great mammals are gone.' It may be that originally larger carnivores might have swallowed the fruit whole, or small rodents might have carried the pits with them to bury elsewhere. Certainly other dispersal systems must have been adequate because the avocado continued to reproduce in the wild until man discovered a taste for it thousands of years ago and began to cultivate it, thus ensuring its survival.

AVOCADO & PRAWN SALAD

SERVES: 4
PREPARATION: 10 MINUTES

The classic pairing of avocado and prawns complement each other perfectly in this simple salad. Enjoy with a glass of crisp white wine.

AVOCADOS ARE KNOWN TO BE A NUTRIENT BOOSTER, WHICH MEANS THEY HELP THE BODY BETTER ABSORB NUTRIENTS IN OTHER VEGETABLES.

INGREDIENTS

- 2 avocados
- 4 tbsp mayonnaise
- 1 tbsp ketchup
- 4 tsp lemon juice
- few drops tabasco sauce
- a pinch of cayenne pepper
- a pinch of smoked paprika
- salt and freshly ground black pepper
- 200g prawns
- Romaine or Cos lettuce

METHOD

Cut the avocados in half and carefully remove the stones. You don't need to peel them. Scoop a little bit more flesh out of the avocado to make a bigger hole.

Combine the mayonnaise, ketchup, lemon juice, tabasco sauce and spices in a bowl and mix thoroughly. Season to taste and toss the prawns in the mixture until thoroughly coated.

Spoon the mixture into the scooped-out avocados and serve with fresh lettuce leaves.

SERVES: 2
PREPARATION: 10 MINUTES

AVOCADO & GRAPEFRUIT SALAD

A light citrussy dressing with the warmth of honey and mustard enhances this tasty pairing of tangy grapefruit and creamy avocado.

INGREDIENTS

- 1 white grapefruit
- 1 pink grapefruit
- 2 ripe avocados
- 30ml extra virgin oil
- 1 tsp honey
- 1 tsp ground mustard

METHOD

Prepare the grapefruit by removing the peel and then carefully remove each slice from the white pith and membrane. Squeeze the juice from the discarded membranes and catch any run-off from your preparation, so that you have around 30ml of juice.

Peel and cut the avocados into long thin slices.

Combine the olive oil, honey and mustard with the grapefruit juice and toss the sliced avocados in the mixture until well coated.

Arrange the grapefruit and avocado slices alternately on a plate and pour over the remaining dressing.

CLASSIC GUACAMOLE

The most famous and widely-enjoyed avocado recipe. Guacamole can be added to a wrap or sandwich, or served as a dip, perfect with tortillas or crunchy vegetables for a genuine taste of Mexico.

INGREDIENTS

- 3 ripe avocados
- 2 ripe tomatoes
- 1 red onion, finely chopped
- juice of 1 lime
- a bunch of coriander
- salt and freshly ground black pepper

METHOD

Peel the avocados, remove the stones and scoop out the flesh.

Combine all the ingredients in a pestle and mortar or food processor until they form a smooth paste, or for a more textured version chop the ingredients together finely.
Season to taste.

Chill for an hour before serving and scatter a few coriander leaves over to garnish.

You can add chillies, garlic or cayenne pepper to the mix for your own twist on this classic recipe.

THE CALIFORNIA AVOCADO COMMISSION ESTIMATED 63,000,000 KILOS OF AVOCADOS WERE CONSUMED AT THE SUPERBOWL IN 2016.

SERVES: 4
PREPARATION: 10 MINUTES

AVOCADO, CHICKEN & BACON WRAP

A delicious alternative to a sandwich, this wrap combines chicken and avocado with the smoky taste of bacon and fresh crisp lettuce.

INGREDIENTS

- 1 cooked chicken breast
- 4 rashers of cooked smoked bacon
- 2 tomatoes
- a little gem lettuce, shredded
- ¼ a cucumber, chopped
- 1 avocado
- 4 tbsp mayonnaise
- juice of ½ a lemon
- salt and freshly ground black pepper
- 4 tortilla wraps

METHOD

Chop the chicken into small chunks and the bacon into small pieces. Slice the tomatoes and combine in a bowl with the lettuce, cucumber, chicken pieces and bacon. Peel and chop the avocado and add to the bowl with the mayonnaise and lemon juice. Toss all the ingredients together and season to taste.

Warm the tortillas for a few minutes. Spread the mixture on to each wrap and wrap up securely.

Eat immediately!

AVOCADO OIL

Avocado oil is extracted from the flesh of the fruit, unlike many other oils which are extracted from seeds. Around 70% of the oil consists of healthy monosaturated fat, and it is loaded with all the other nutrients and antioxidants of the avocado, making it arguably one of the most beneficial oils to use in our diet.

Avocado oil has a smooth nutty flavour which makes it a great salad or drizzling oil, but what is less well-recognised is that it is an excellent cooking oil due to its stability when heated. When oils reach a certain temperature they begin to smoke, and then to break down, not only losing nutritional value in the process but actually beginning to create unhealthy compounds. Avocado oil has a very high 'smoke point' of around 270°C – significantly higher than other oils including olive oil.

Cold-pressed avocado oil is increasingly being used topically in many beauty treatments as well. Skin needs collagen to retain its elasticity and youthfulness, and the nutrients in avocados stimulate collagen production. Avocado oil is a carrier oil, which means it soaks deep into the skin, and for this reason it is often used as a base for massage oils, particularly for dry and sensitive skins. Studies have shown that avocado oil has the best penetration rate and the best sun-protection factor among natural oils. The humectants in the avocado help retain moisture for longer, thus keeping skin smooth and wrinkle-free and protecting against the effects of ageing.

Avocado oil can help with medical skin conditions too such as psoriasis, excema, sunburn and even nappy rash. It has also been used to heal minor wounds, as the oleic acid and other essential fatty acids aid skin renewal while inflammation is reduced.

With uses ranging from beauty and skincare, to hair and scalp treatments and even as an oil for treating wood, avocado oil is becoming more and more popular.

CHEESECAKE

SERVES: 4
PREPARATION: 20 MINUTES

Zingy lemon and creamy avocado combine with a rich crunchy ginger base in this easy no-cook recipe for cheesecake. You can decorate the top using grated dark chocolate or pistachio nuts instead of the lime zest if you prefer.

AVOCADOS HAVE A HIGH FAT CONTENT. IT IS, HOWEVER, MONO-SATURATED FAT. THIS HELPS REDUCE HIGH CHOLESTEROL LEVELS AND LOWERS THE RISK OF HEART DISEASE AND STROKES.

INGREDIENTS

For the base:
- 50g unsalted butter
- 200g ginger biscuits

For the filling:
- 4 ripe avocados
- 2 tbsp coconut oil, melted
- 2 tbsp lime juice
- 2 tbsp agave syrup
- zest of 1 lime

For the topping:
- 125g cream cheese
- 50g butter
- 300g icing sugar
- 1 tsp vanilla essence

METHOD

Melt the butter. Crush the ginger biscuits into fine crumbs, and combine with the butter. Place the mix into a spring-form cake tin and flatten down to form a base. Chill for half an hour.

Blend the avocados with the oil and lime juice until a smooth paste is formed. Stir the agave syrup through and add half of the lime zest. Spread the filling evenly over the biscuit base.

Combine the cream cheese, butter, icing sugar and vanilla essence, then spread evenly on top of the filling.

Decorate the cheesecake with the remaining lime zest. Return the cheesecake to the fridge to chill for another half an hour before serving.

SERVES: 2
PREPARATION: 5 MINUTES

COCKTAILS

Avocados add a sophisticated creamy twist to these two classic cocktail recipes.

INGREDIENTS

- 2 limes
- 60ml tequila
- 30ml Cointreau
- ½ ripe avocado
- 1 tsp agave syrup
- 1 tbsp chopped coriander leaves
- pinch of cayenne pepper
- crushed ice
- salt for coating the rim of your glass

MARGARITA

Squeeze 1½ of the limes to get around 30ml of juice. Slice the final half of the lime thinly and keep all the leftover peel. Add the lime juice to the remaining ingredients and whizz until smooth in a blender. Rub the rims of two glasses with the lime peel before dipping into the salt. Once coated, pour the cocktail into the glasses. Garnish with a slice of lime.

INGREDIENTS

- 100ml light rum
- 15ml lemon juice
- 15ml lime juice
- 50ml agave syrup
- ¼ ripe avocado
- 15ml cream
- ice

DAQUIRI

The quintessential rum cocktail from Cuba, the daquiri works perfectly with a smooth avocado base. Just blend all the ingredients and enjoy!

HEALTH & BEAUTY

*'... the avocado
is a food without
rival among the fruits,
the veritable fruit
of paradise.'*

David Fairchild
(1869–1954),
American botanist
and plant explorer

FACIAL TREATMENTS

The vitamins in avocados are great for boosting skin moisture and keeping wrinkles at bay.

INGREDIENTS

- 1 ripe avocado
- 1 tsp honey

 TOP TIP

You can add oatmeal to your face mask to create a gentle scrub, or an egg white to combat oily skin. If you have very dry skin add a couple of drops of olive oil for extra moisturising.

FACE MASK

Enjoy a totally natural beauty treatment with this easy face mask recipe.

Peel the avocado (keep the peel for the treatment below). Mash with a teaspoon of honey using a pestle and mortar until you have a smooth paste.

Slather on your face, relax and leave on for as long as possible – at least 15 minutes – before gently rinsing off.

AVOCADO PEEL TREATMENT

The peel of the avocado is rich in oils containing a substance called humectant. You can apply it directly to your face in this simple treatment.

Scrape off any remaining pulp from the peel, and using it like a face cloth, sweep the soft side of the peel over your face in circular movements. Gently massage for 30 seconds and wash off with warm water and a muslin cloth. Even better, leave the oils on overnight before rinsing off.

BATH OIL

Turn an ordinary bath into a luxurious spa experience with this gorgeous avocado and essential oils bath treatment. Nourishing, relaxing and moisturizing, for beautifully soft skin and soothed senses.

METHOD

Mix the almond and avocado oils together and warm gently in a pan. Turn off the heat and add two bags of camomile tea.

Once cooled remove the teabags and add the aromatherapy oils until you have a scent you enjoy. Pour the mixture into a glass bottle and leave for a day to steep.

Pour sparingly into your bath, lie back, breathe in the relaxing scent and let the sensuous mix of ingredients work their magic.

INGREDIENTS

- 200ml almond oil
- 400ml avocado oil
- 2 camomile teabags
- a few drops of lavender oil, rose oil or other essential scent of your choice

AVOCADO OIL IS RICH IN ESSENTIAL MINERALS AND VITAMINS. PARTICULARLY VITAMINS A. D AND E. AS A CARRIER OIL IT SOAKS INTO THE SKIN REALLY WELL.

AVOCADO CAPITAL OF THE WORLD

The Americans have a full-blown love affair with the avocado, and luckily the climate in the states of Florida and California is perfect for growing them on an industrial scale.

90% of the avocados grown in the USA are produced in California, and of these half are grown in San Diego County. A single California avocado tree can produce around 500 avocados a year.

The small town of Fallbrook in San Diego County is one of the biggest growers of avocados and claims the title of 'Avocado capital of the world', with a welcome sign proudly featuring a giant avocado.

Each year around 10,000 visitors come to Fallbrook for the annual Avocado Festival, which elevates the avocado to a work of art and a source of entertainment as hundreds of enthusiasts gather to celebrate the fruit.

Here you can find craft stalls selling furniture made of avocado wood, booths selling just about anything you can eat that is avocado-based, and demonstrations of avocado cooking. For the more artistic there is an Art of the Avocado Contest with works of art on display to be judged by popular choice.

In addition there is a wide range of competitions. Prizes are given for the largest avocado, the best

guacamole, the best decorated avocado and, for the kids, a 'Little Miss and Mr Avocado' contest. There is avocado ice cream, 'Holy Guaca-Moly' booths, carniaval rides

> *There is an Avocado 500 car race where children have to build and race cars made out of avocados.*

and a giant inflatable avocado, not to mention the 'Avocado 500' car race where children have to build and race cars made out of avocados ...

However, Fallbrook is not the only claimant to this title. Both the cities of Uruapan and Tancítaro in Mexico consider themselves to be the 'authentic' avocado capital of the world. In 2013 the college students in Tancítaro entered the Guinness World Book of Records for creating the largest serving of guacamole ever, weighing a staggering 2,669.5kg!

HAND TREATMENT

For beautiful hands try this home-made treatment. The humectants in the avocado oil seal in moisture while the lemon juice cleanses your skin and strengthens brittle nails.

METHOD

Mash up the avocado and add the oil gradually. Add the lemon to provide a lovely citrus scent. Massage into your hands and leave on for 15 minutes before rinsing off gently.

You can also treat age spots with avocado oil due to the presence of a type of natural steroid called sterolin which helps to moisturise skin. Mix up an equal amount of avocado oil and castor oil for a deeply moisturising hand treatment.

INGREDIENTS

- 1 ripe avocado
- 1 tbsp olive oil
- 1 tsp lemon juice

 TOP TIP

For the best results, apply at bedtime. Slip on some cotton manicure gloves and leave the treatment to soak in overnight.

EXFOLIANT

There are nutritionalists who claim that you can grind up the avocado stone and eat it, but there is some discussion over whether this is beneficial. After all, it was designed to be swallowed whole by prehistoric sloths, not chewed! However, there are other uses for the discarded stone. Here, the ground-up stone provides a natural exfoliant in this simple recipe.

💡 TOP TIP

Many shop-bought scrubs contain environmentally harmful plastic microbeads, which add to ocean pollution and are damaging to sea-life. Using a natural scrub instead is great for your skin and the environment!

METHOD

Remove the stone from an avocado, wash clean and leave to dry out completely – this should take three to five days. Then cut your stone carefully into quarters and blend into a fine grit in a food processor.

Mix the blended stone grit with half a ripe avocado, the coconut oil and lemon juice. Gently massage into your skin. Rinse well and enjoy your super-smooth complexion.

INGREDIENTS

- 1 avocado stone
- ½ ripe avocado
- 1 tsp coconut oil
- 1 tsp lemon juice

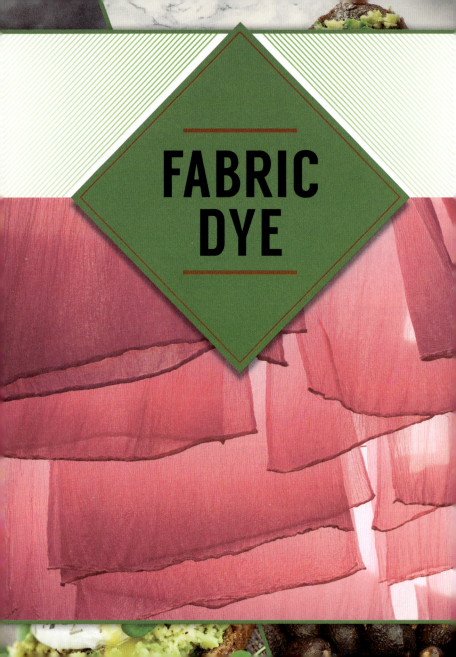

FABRIC DYE

YOU WILL NEED:

- a large saucepan
- 4 or 5 avocado stones, thoroughly cleaned
- steel tongs
- some pH neutral detergent
- rubber gloves

Avocados can be used in a huge range of recipes and beauty treatments. But what should you do with all those discarded avocado stones?

Here's how you can recycle avocado stones by using them to create a beautiful natural dye. Avocado stones contain tannin which helps colour bind to fabric. It works best with natural fibres such as cotton. The resulting colour will be a pale peachy-pink, with different depths of colour depending on the fabric.

 TOP TIP

pH neutral means that on a scale of 1–14, the detergent scores a mid-range 7 (1 being the most acidic and 14 being the most alkaline). Most laundry detergents are rated at 9, but you can find eco-friendly or delicate wash options with a neutral rating.

You will want to experiment with different materials and lengths of immersion in the dye to get the effect you prefer. Wash the fabric you want to dye thoroughly and soak in hot water overnight. Fill the saucepan with water and add the avocado stones. Bring the water to the boil and simmer gently for about 20 minutes until the colour is released from the stones. It will be light pink to begin with but will gradually darken.

When the colour is dark enough add the fabric and agitate it for several minutes with the tongs so the colour is evenly absorbed. Leave to soak for at least an hour. The longer you leave the fabric in the dye the richer the colour will be. Remove the material and rinse in warm water with the pH neutral detergent before hanging up to dry.

HEAD & HAIR

Avocado oil is perfect for dry hair as it can be absorbed by the shafts.
Use as a massage oil for hair and scalp.

METHOD

Create a treatment for strong shiny hair by mixing a small amount of avocado and olive oil with the white of an egg and some honey. Leave on your hair for five to ten minutes before rinsing off.

Dandruff can be treated by regularly massaging the scalp with a warmed mix of avocado oil and castor oil. If possible leave overnight, for beautifully soft hair and a dandruff-free scalp.

INGREDIENTS

- 1 tbsp avocado oil
- 1 tbsp olive oil
- 1 egg white
- 1 tsp honey

 TOP TIP

Using Manuka honey (which contains excellent hair-repair properties) in this treatment, is great for repairing split ends and protecting against future damage.

GROW YOUR OWN

Growing a beautiful baby avocado tree from an avocado stone is simple, and it is fascinating to see how plants regenerate from seed. Don't get too excited about harvesting your own fruit just yet though as it can take up to five years for the tree to produce any!

Remove the stone from the avocado very carefully so that it is intact. Wash it gently to remove any of the remaining flesh without damaging the brown skin.

Now you need to identify which way up your stone is. Most avocado stones are oval although some can be more rounded in shape. The bottom end will be slightly flattened and the top end slightly pointed. The roots will grow from the bottom and the leaves from the top so it is important to get this right.

Insert a few toothpicks firmly into the side of the stone so that it can be suspended over a see-through container of water.

Make sure that an inch of water covers the bottom half of the stone. Place the container in a warm place away from direct sunlight.

Within a few weeks (anywhere between three to eight) you should see roots forming in the water and a shoot emerging from the top of the stone.

It is essential to keep the roots submerged and to change the water every week to prevent mould and bacteria forming.

When the shoot reaches a height of around 15cm, cut it back to 6cm to stimulate growth.

Once it reaches 15cm again, it is ready to be repotted. Plant it in a rich composted soil with the top of the pit exposed and water regularly. When the shoot reaches 30cm, cut it back to 15cm. Each time the shoot reaches this height, pinch out the top two shoots to encourage a bushy side growth.

Avocado trees are best grown in warm temperatures, so if you plant your baby tree outside you will need to bring it indoors in cold periods. It will need frequent watering too while it establishes itself. After that all you need is patience ...

CONVERSION CHART
FOR COMMON MEASUREMENTS

LIQUIDS

15 ml	½ fl oz
25 ml	1 fl oz
50 ml	2 fl oz
75 ml	3 fl oz
100 ml	3 ½ fl oz
125 ml	4 fl oz
150 ml	¼ pint
175 ml	6 fl oz
200 ml	7 fl oz
250 ml	8 fl oz
275 ml	9 fl oz
300 ml	½ pint
325 ml	11 fl oz
350 ml	12 fl oz
375 ml	13 fl oz
400 ml	14 fl oz
450 ml	¾ pint
475 ml	16 fl oz
500 ml	17 fl oz
575 ml	18 fl oz
600 ml	1 pint
750 ml	1 ¼ pints
900 ml	1 ½ pints
1 litre	1 ¾ pints
1.2 litres	2 pints
1.5 litres	2 ½ pints
1.8 litres	3 pints
2 litres	3 ½ pints
2.5 litres	4 pints
3.6 litres	6 pints

WEIGHTS

5 g	¼ oz
15 g	½ oz
20 g	¾ oz
25 g	1 oz
50 g	2 oz
75 g	3 oz
125 g	4 oz
150 g	5 oz
175 g	6 oz
200 g	7 oz
250 g	8 oz
275 g	9 oz
300 g	10 oz
325 g	11 oz
375 g	12 oz
400 g	13 oz
425 g	14 oz
475 g	15 oz
500 g	1 lb
625 g	1 ¼ lb
750 g	1 ½ lb
875 g	1 ¾ lb
1 kg	2 lb
1.25 kg	2 ½ lb
1.5 kg	3 lb
1.75 kg	3 ½ lb
2 kg	4 lb

OVEN TEMPERATURES

110°C .... (225°F) .... gas mark ¼
120°C .... (250°F) .... gas mark ½
140°C .... (275°F) .... gas mark 1
150°C .... (300°F) .... gas mark 2
160°C .... (325°F) .... gas mark 3
180°C .... (350°F) .... gas mark 4
190°C .... (375°F) .... gas mark 5
200°C ...... (400°F) .... gas mark 6
220°C ...... (425°F) .... gas mark 7
230°C ...... (450°F) .... gas mark 8

MEASUREMENTS

5 mm .... ¼ inch
1 cm .... ½ inch
1.5 cm .... ¾ inch
2.5 cm .... 1 inch
5 cm .... 2 inches
7 cm .... 3 inches
10 cm .... 4 inches
12 cm .... 5 inches
15 cm .... 6 inches
18 cm .... 7 inches
20 cm .... 8 inches
23 cm .... 9 inches
25 cm .... 10 inches
28 cm .... 11 inches
30 cm .... 12 inches
33 cm .... 13 inches

KEY TO SYMBOLS

(DF) Dairy free

(GF) Gluten free

(V) Vegetarian

(VG) Vegan

A NOTE ON USING DIFFERENT OVENS

Not all ovens are the same, and the more cooking you do the better you will get to know yours. If a recipe says that you need to bake something for ten minutes or until golden brown, use your judgment as to whether it needs a few extra minutes. Conversely don't overcook food by following the timings rigidly if you think it looks ready.

As a general rule gas ovens have more uneven heat distribution so the top of the oven may be hotter than the bottom. Electric ovens tend to maintain a regular temperature throughout and distribute heat more evenly, especially fan ovens.

All the recipes in this book have been tested in an electric oven with a fan. Recommended oven temperatures are provided for electric (Celsius and Fahrenheit), and gas. If you have a fan oven then lower the electric temperature by 20°.

Bloomsbury Publishing
An imprint of Bloomsbury Publishing plc

50 Bedford Square
London
WC1B 3DP
UK

1385 Broadway
New York
NY 10018
USA

www.bloomsbury.com

BLOOMSBURY and the Diana logo are trademarks of Bloomsbury Publishing Plc

First Published in 2017

© Bloomsbury Publishing plc

Created for Bloomsbury by Plum5 Ltd

Photographs and Illustrations © Shutterstock

All rights reserved. No part of this publication may be reproduced or transmitted in any form or
by any means, electronic or mechanical, including photocopying, recording, or any information
storage or retrieval system, without prior permission in writing from the publishers.

No responsibility for loss caused to any individual or organization acting on
or refraining from action as a result of the material in this publication can be accepted
by Bloomsbury or the author.

British Library Cataloguing-in-Publication Data

A catalogue record for this book is available from the British Library.

Library of Congress Cataloguing-in-Publication Data

A catalogue record for this book is available from the Library of Congress.

ISBN: 9781408887141

2 4 6 8 10 9 7 5 3 1

Printed in China by C&C Printing

To find out more about our authors and books visit www.bloomsbury.com.
Here you will find extracts, author interviews, details of forthcoming events
and the option to sign up for our newsletters.